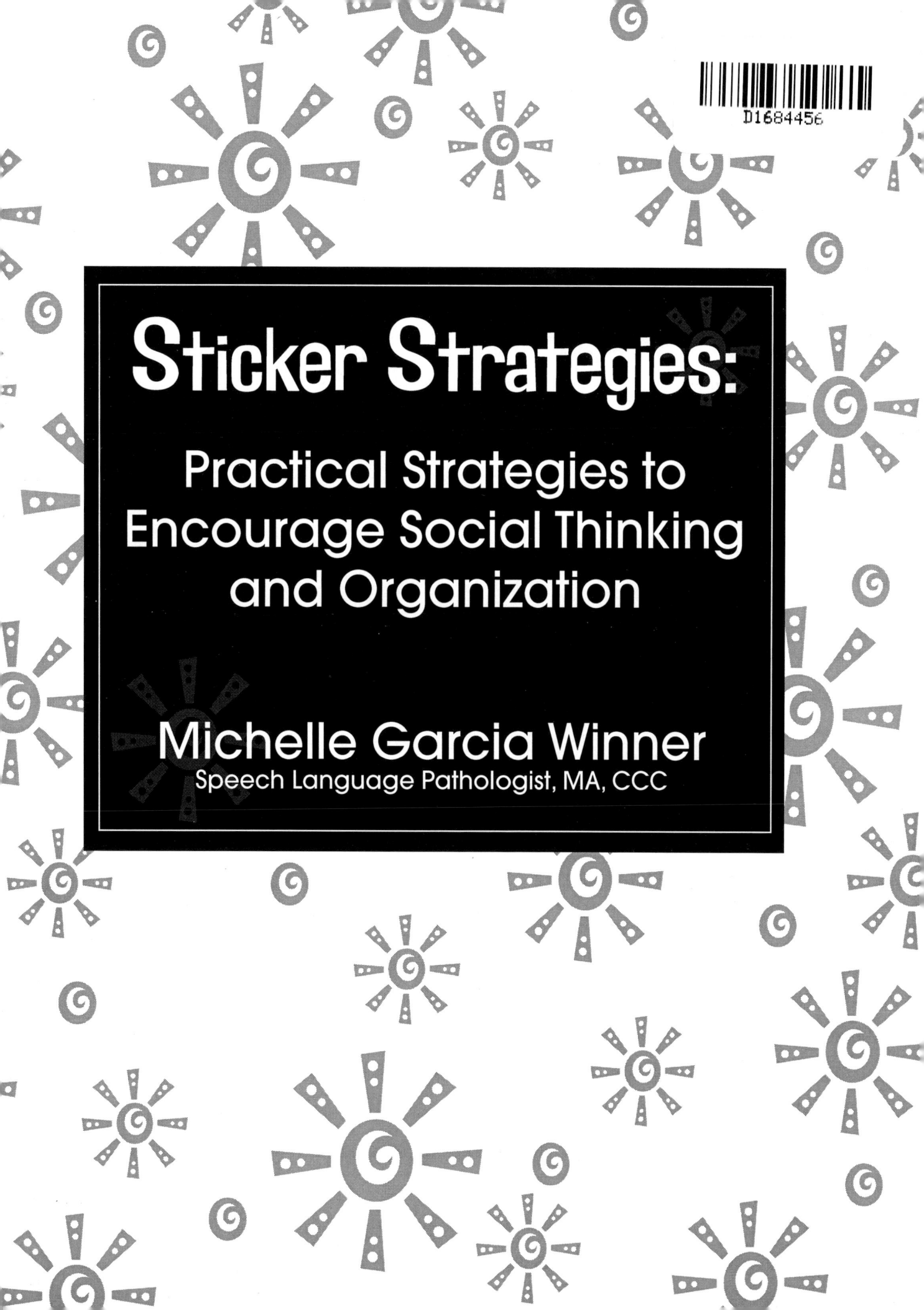

Sticker Strategies:
Practical Strategies to Encourage
Social Thinking and Organization
2nd Edition

By Michelle Garcia Winner
Speech Language Pathologist, MA, CCC

Think Social Publishing, Inc.
3031 Tisch Way, Suite 800
San Jose, CA 95128
Phone (408) 557-8595
Toll-Free (877) 464-9278
Fax (408) 557-8594
Information@socialthinking.com

www.socialthinking.com

Copyright©2010, Michelle Garcia Winner
All rights reserved. This book cannot be copied for the purposes of re-sale or sharing as an entire product.
Pages in this book can be copied for the purposes of educating students and other professionals.

Library of Congress Control Number: 2010930330
ISBN: 978-0-9825231-4-8

Note to reader: this book is intended to provide ideas of how to develop succinct strategies to teach to students. The reader is encouraged to develop their own strategies to meet the needs of specific students to go along with those included in this book.

Cover and text design and layout by Elizabeth A. Blacker.
This book is printed and bound in California by Medius Corporation.

To order copies of this book, please visit www.socialthinking.com.

Acknowledgements:

A big thank you to Maxer, his family, and his parapros who worked closely with me on developing the idea of social thinking strategy cards.

…and to Erika, Sasha, Tamsin, Kristy, Kristen, Benjamin, Anna and all my other clients who have kept me "real" all these years while teaching me how to teach them how to create strategies.

Sticker Strategy Table of Contents:

Introduction vi

Asking for Help (AH) 1
I need help 2
I need clarification 2
I need help 3
I'm stuck 3
I need a brain break 4
I will ask for help by… 4
Help me strategies 5
Remembering to thank people who help 5
Blank card 6

Emotions and Problem Solving (EPS) 7
My system is shutting down 8
Smooth sailing 8
My move it strategy! 9
Calm Down Reminders 10
Calming Down Strategies 10
I need a break 11
Learning about my calm and stress:
5 point scale 11
The Size of my Problem 12
Emotional Expression Compression 12
Emotional Expression Compression cont. 13
Making my own Problem/Emotion Index 13
The Size of My Problem 14
Solving Problems before they become
Big Problems 14
Becoming Successful: Working Towards a Goal 15
Making my Own Success: Step by Step 15
I Need a Break 16
Emotion Summary 16
Emotions 17
Emotions are Contagious 17
We all have Emotions, but in the Classroom… 18
The Spirals of Failure and Success 18
The Spiral of Social Failure 19
The Spiral of Social Success 19
Blank card 20

Organization, Writing and Homework (O) .. 21
Line-Thought: Strategy for Brainstorming 22
Get Started by… 22
Getting School Stuff Ready to Take Home 23
Getting Started on Homework Once Home 23
Getting My Mind Organized to Start to
do Homework 24
Starting to do the Homework 24
Homework Time is Set: Free Time and
Upset Time are Flexible 25
Breaking my Homework Assignments Down 25
Breaking my Homework Assignments Down 26
Why we Predict Time 26
Make a Game of Predicting Time 27
Turning Homework In 27
Why Turn Homework In? 28
Who Feels Good when my Homework is Done? 28
My Work and Break Card 29
Blank card 29

Group Work (GW) 31
Working in a Group and Being with People 32
Starters for Working in a Group 32
Pointless Work 33
Thinking about Social Behavior Mapping 33
Boring Moment Expectations 34
Doing What is Unexpected when I am Having
A Boring Moment 34
Blank card 35

Social Thinking (ST) 37
Being Social 38
From Friendly to Friendship 38
Levels of Friendship .... 39 - 40
When do we use Social Skills? 40
The 4 steps of Social Thinking/Perspective Taking 41
Perspective Taking-Step 1 41
Perspective Taking-Step 2 42
Perspective Taking-Step 3 42
Perspective Taking-Step 4 43
Social Emotional Memory 43
Feelings Count 44
Calling People even if you have Phone Anxiety 44
The 4 Steps of Communication 45
Communication-Step 1 45
Communication-Step 2 46
Communication-Step 3 46
Communication-Step 4 47
Blank card 47

Family Time – Home Strategies (FT) 49
Family Dinner Time: Answering Questions 50
Family Dinner Time: Asking Questions 50
Family Dinner Time: Add your own Thoughts 51
After Dinner is Done: Help Out 51
Sharing the TV 52
Sharing the TV 52
Ending an Activity when Asked 53
Getting Ready for Bed 53
People Think about how you Smell 54
Getting up in the Morning 54
Morning Routine 55
Parents are People Too 55
Apologizing 56
Social Memories of Parents 56
Taking my Medications 57
Life is Not Fair 57
Doing chores 58
Making my chores routine 58
Blank card 59

Sticker Strategies: Practical Strategies to Encourage Social Thinking and Organization

Introduction:

This product was developed after I realized a few very important points about being an effective teacher for persons with social cognitive learning challenges:

1. Nagging does not teach.
2. Students have to choose which teaching strategies work for them.
3. Students have to "own" their own strategies.
4. Students have to learn to locate their strategies by themselves.
5. Students must feel proud of their individual accomplishments rather than feel they are just doing what they are told to do.

This is a product of color-coded strategies (if printed out on a color printer) to help take ownership for the strategies they are learning and be more organized allowing them to function across the environments of home and school.

The strategies are organized by the following topics, each topic is represented by a different color sticker on the CD:

1. Asking for Help (AH)
2. Emotions and Problem Solving (EPS)
3. Organization, Writing and Homework (OWH)
4. Group Work (GW)
5. Social Thinking (ST)
6. Family Time – Home Strategies (FT)

Putting the strategies onto Stickers to stick in a strategy based notebook:

1. You need to purchase a spiral-bind set of index cards, size 4x6 inches.
2. You will also need to purchase the Avery sticker labels mentioned below.
3. You will need to purchase the self-adhesive index labels.

This product was revised in 2010 to keep pace with technology and to cut back on the price of the book. The original version contained actual stickers but this made the book very expensive. We modified the book to put all the sticker strategies onto a CD disc for the user to have the choice as to whether they want to download them onto sticker labels to print out or to embed them into some other type of strategy notebook created on the computer.

A low tech solution for placing the strategies on spiral bound index cards:
A very low-tech solution is simply to copy on a Xerox machine the strategies that are provided in black and white in the pages of this book and cut and tape them into a spiral bound index card-set.

To use the CD attached to the book to print out colored strategies onto paper or sticker labels:

To place the strategies onto a sticker based label, we recommend you purchase the Avery labels mentioned below, although other products may suffice as well.

1. Purchase 5168 (for laser printer) or 8168 (for Ink-jet printer).
2. Once you have the labels available continue with the following steps:

To use the Avery template included on the CD:

3. Put the CD attached to this book into your computer and open the contents of the CD.
4. Open the file called "Avery5168-8168.doc" in your Microsoft Word program. (Avery.com has templates for different programs on their website available for free download.)
5. Click inside one of the label spaces to place a strategy.

6. To choose a strategy:
   a. Choose "Insert picture from file" from the menu and migrate to the strategy on the CD that you would like to insert. For example, if you would like to use the "I Need Help" strategy on page 2 of this book, you would open the folder called "Asking For Help" and select the file called "AH1.jpg" to place into the template.
7. Repeat steps 5 and 6 until all of the spaces are filled with strategies you have selected.
8. Insert your labels into your printer, following the label directions.
9. Print using Avery labels 5168 (for laser printer) or 8168 (for Ink-jet printer).

To use the CD attached to the book to print out black and white strategies onto paper or sticker labels:

Follow steps 1 through 8 above.
9. Select File/Print from the Microsoft Word menu.
10. Select Paper Type/Quality
11. Select Grayscale
12. Print using Avery labels 5168 (for laser printer) or 8168 (for Ink-jet printer).

Or
9. Print directly to a black and white printer.

Placing stickers onto spiral bound index cards (See illustraton):

1. Organize your spiral bound index cards into sections using sticky back tabs you can purchase from office supply stores.
   a. Write the name of each section on one of the tabs, etc.
   b. If your student is highly visual, color code the tabs for the student to more quickly recognize the way in which the cards are organized.

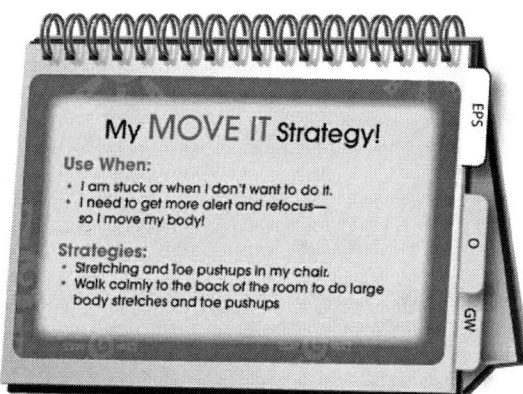

2. Use the topics indicated above to divide the spiral-bind index cards into up to these 6 sections (you can choose to make less sections, or add your own section as well).
   a. If you are creating 6 sections, then approximately divide the index cards into 6 sections, roughly allowing for an equal number of cards to be in each section. E.g. if there are 60 cards on the spiral bind, then allow 10 cards in each section.
   b. As you add your stickers into the spiral binder, place each sticker into its relevant section. This allows the student and teacher to most easily locate the strategies at the moment they are needed.

This illustration demonstrates what this spiral bound set of strategies looks like.

To learn more about how you might use the Sticker Strategies in context, refer to information written about the ME BINDER in my book *Thinking About You Thinking About Me*, 2007.

This product is not a cookbook!

There is no limit to the number of strategies a teacher or parent can create and there is no requirement to how many strategies a student must use to use this product well. It is always best to start with less strategies for a student to practice using these cards at time of need, than overwhelming him or her right away with too many strategies! You can always add more strategies as the student develops more abilty to handle new information.

There is a range of ideas represented in the strategy stickers. The parent and/or professional must decide which strategies are the most relevant for the student and then the student decides which strategies he or she is willing to use. There is a difference between what we think a student should be taught and what a student is willing to learn. Giving the student a choice helps him/her to feel like they are in the center of their treatment program, rather than having to submit blindly to professional or parental persuasion.

This is a launching pad:

The sticker strategies provided within this resource will undoubtedly trigger you, the parent/professional, to modify or come up with your own ideas. PLEASE DO. Feel free to create your strategy ideas on the blank stickers available on the CD, or make your own set of strategies by just writing them on index cards. Like all of my products, I hope this product is just more "food for thought." Enjoy the process. Enjoy these remarkable students who teach us so much about ourselves.

Asking For Help
(AH)

Sticker Strategies: Practical Strategies to Encourage Social Thinking and Organization

AH1.jpg

I need help.

©2010 Michelle Garcia Winner   www.socialthinking.com

AH2.jpg

I need clarification.

Please check with me to make sure I know what to do.

©2010 Michelle Garcia Winner   www.socialthinking.com

Asking For Help

AH3.jpg

I NEED HELP!

↓   ↓   ↓

On **PART** of it.   On **MOST** of it.   On **ALL** of it.

©2010 Michelle Garcia Winner   www.socialthinking.com

AH4.jpg

I'm Stuck!

I don't want to do this.	I don't know how to do this.

©2010 Michelle Garcia Winner   www.socialthinking.com

Copyright©2010, Michelle Garcia Winner
All rights reserved. This book cannot be copied for the purposes of re-sale or sharing as an entire product.
This page may be copied for the purposes of educating students and other professionals.

Sticker Strategies: Practical Strategies to Encourage Social Thinking and Organization

AH5.jpg

I need a brain break!

Please give me a few minutes to get my brain organized.

©2010 Michelle Garcia Winner   www.socialthinking.com

AH6.jpg

I will ask for help by…

_____

(Write your strategy here)
- Raising my hand.
- Showing my sticker strategy.
- Standing next to my teacher's desk.

©2010 Michelle Garcia Winner   www.socialthinking.com

Copyright©2010, Michelle Garcia Winner
All rights reserved. This book cannot be copied for the purposes of re-sale or sharing as an entire product.
This page may be copied for the purposes of educating students and other professionals.

AH7.jpg

Help Me Strategies...

Use When: I don't Know how to do the assignment and I am feeling anxious.

Strategies:

- I calm myself by_____
- I ask for help by _____
- I remember the teacher has other people to help at the same time, so I have to be patient!

©2010 Michelle Garcia Winner   www.socialthinking.com

AH8.jpg

Remembering to Thank People who HELP.

People like to help other people. It makes each of us feel good to be able to help another person.

People like it when you show or tell them that you appreciate them. People feel good about you when you show people that you are glad they took the time to be with you.

You can say "thank you" in many different ways:
- Smile
- Say "thanks."
- Say "that really helped."
- Say "goodbye" in a friendly tone of voice.

©2010 Michelle Garcia Winner   www.socialthinking.com

Sticker Strategies: Practical Strategies to Encourage Social Thinking and Organization

AH-Blank.jpg

©2010 Michelle Garcia Winner　　　　www.socialthinking.com

EPS1.jpg

My System is
shutting down.

I need to
get up and **move.**

©2010 Michelle Garcia Winner	www.socialthinking.com

EPS2.jpg

Smooth Sailing…

All is going
well enough!

©2010 Michelle Garcia Winner	www.socialthinking.com

EPS1.jpg

My System is
shutting down.

I need to
get up and **move.**

©2010 Michelle Garcia Winner www.socialthinking.com

EPS2.jpg

Smooth Sailing…

All is going
well enough!

©2010 Michelle Garcia Winner www.socialthinking.com

Emotions and Problem Solving

EPS3.jpg

My MOVE IT Strategy!

Use When:
- I am stuck or when I don't want to do it.
- I need to get more alert and refocus— so I move my body!

Strategies:
- Stretching and toe pushups in my chair.
- Walk calmly to the back of the room to do large body stretches and toe pushups

©2010 Michelle Garcia Winner	www.socialthinking.com

EPS4.jpg

My MOVE IT Strategy!

Use When:
- I am stuck or when I don't want to do it.
- I need to get more alert and refocus— so I move my body!

Strategies:

- _____
- _____
- _____

©2010 Michelle Garcia Winner	www.socialthinking.com

EPS5.jpg

Calm Down Reminders:

- By staying calm, it is easier to get my brain to focus.
- Doing some work is better than doing no work.
- Teachers are here to help.
- No one understands everything that they are taught.
- If I can try to explain my problem, people get a better idea of how to help me.
- Most students don't really like doing school work, even if they are not complaining.

©2010 Michelle Garcia Winner   www.socialthinking.com

EPS6.jpg

Calming Down Strategies:

When I need to calm down, I will use the following strategies:

1. Breath slowly
2. Try to relax my hands, then my arms, etc…

3. _____

4. _____

5. _____

©2010 Michelle Garcia Winner   www.socialthinking.com

Emotions and Problem Solving

EPS7.jpg

I Need a Break:

I really need to stop working for a few minutes and take a break. Once my body and brain calm back down I will rejoin the group and get back to work.

During my break I can go to _____

I can do the following things _____

I need to avoid _____

©2010 Michelle Garcia Winner   www.socialthinking.com

EPS8.jpg

Learning about my Calm and Stress:

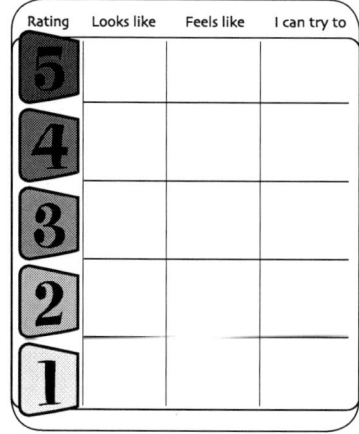

My Incredible 5 point scale

(Buron-Dunn, Curtis, 2004)

©2010 Michelle Garcia Winner   www.socialthinking.com

Copyright©2010, Michelle Garcia Winner
All rights reserved. This book cannot be copied for the purposes of re-sale or sharing as an entire product.
This page may be copied for the purposes of educating students and other professionals.

EPS9.jpg

The Size of my Problem:

The size of my problem should be related to the size of my emotions about the problem.

Problem:		Emotional Reaction:
• Crisis	10 →	Very upset
• Someone played a mean trick on me	7 →	Sad and Frustrated and Angry
• Someone yelled at me	5 →	Mad
• My schedule changed	2 →	Irritated
• No real problem just aren't perfect	1 →	Calm

©2010 Michelle Garcia Winner   www.socialthinking.com

EPS10.jpg

Emotional Expression Compression:

As we get older we are expected to act like we are maintaining a sense of calm even when we are upset.

That means, the size of your problem no longer directly matches the size of your emotion!

If you feel a size 5, 7 or 8 problem you are supposed to react like it is a size 3 problem.

In middle school and certainly by high school we are supposed to appear to stay cool, calm and collected even when we feel enormous stress and unhappiness.

©2010 Michelle Garcia Winner   www.socialthinking.com

Emotions and Problem Solving

EPS11.jpg

Emotional Expression Compression:

The words we use may not convey how truly upset we are. If we are really mad, and someone asks how we are doing, you might just say "I am not having the best day" or "I'm a little frustrated" while saying it with a pretty calm voice and face.

If you are a teenager or young adult at school or in the community and you are yelling, looking furious this is unexpected behavior. People will worry that you are going to hurt them or perhaps yourself.

©2010 Michelle Garcia Winner   www.socialthinking.com

EPS12.jpg

Making my own Problem/Emotion Index:

The size of my problem should be related to the size of my emotions about the problem.

Write in a Problem:	Write in a related Emotional Reaction:
• _____ →	• _____
• _____ →	• _____
• _____ →	• _____
• _____ →	• _____
• _____ →	• _____

©2010 Michelle Garcia Winner   www.socialthinking.com

Sticker Strategies: Practical Strategies to Encourage Social Thinking and Organization

EPS13.jpg

The Size of My Problem:

Problems come in different sizes. I have to practice recognizing the size of my problem should connect to the size of my emotion.

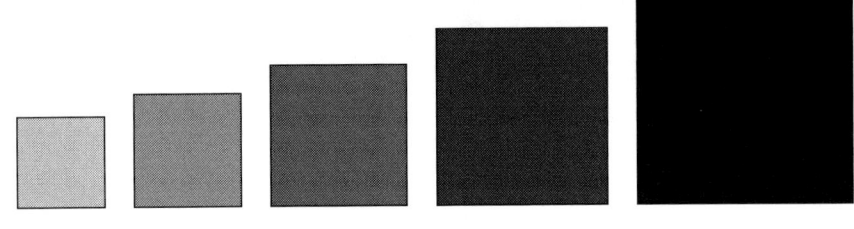

©2010 Michelle Garcia Winner   www.socialthinking.com

EPS14.jpg

Solving Problems before they become Big Problems

Problems come in different sizes. Problems are like bacteria, they increase in size and number if ignored. I need to recognize I have a problem and create a plan to try and stop it from getting bigger.

I start by:
1. Recognizing I have a problem...we all have little problems on a daily basis!
2. Figure out my choices for making the problem smaller.
3. Coming up with a plan to follow through with my choice.

I remember:
If I ignore my problem, it will GROW and become an even bigger PROBLEM.

©2010 Michelle Garcia Winner   www.socialthinking.com

Copyright©2010, Michelle Garcia Winner
All rights reserved. This book cannot be copied for the purposes of re-sale or sharing as an entire product.
This page may be copied for the purposes of educating students and other professionals.

Emotions and Problem Solving

EPS15.jpg

Becoming Successful: Working Towards a Goal.

We all should have a goal. A Goal is something you **THINK ABOUT**.

However, if we only talk about our goal and don't do anything differently, we probably won't accomplish our goal. We may become really sad because it feels like things aren't going our way.

In order to work towards a goal we need a plan.
A Plan is something you **DO**… A plan requires an **ACTION**.

A "Check" is how we evaluate our actions towards our goal. We have to "check" to see if we have done the work the way we should.

So…
To be more successful, we need to **THINK** about a **GOAL** and then we need to Create a **PLAN** that we can **DO**. Next, we need to **CHECK** to see if we have done it right. If not, we have to come up with a new **PLAN**.

©2010 Michelle Garcia Winner   www.socialthinking.com

EPS16.jpg

Making my Own Success: Step by Step.

Goals can be large or small. A large goal is graduating from college. A small goal is finishing my homework tonight. It is best to start by working on smaller goals.

My goal is something **I THINK**:	My plan is something **I DO**, it is the activity I do to achieve my Goal.
The goal I think I can achieve is:	The activity I will do to meet my goal is:
_____	_____
	_____
	_____

When I meet my goal I will feel _____. I will also get to

reward myself by doing _____, when my goal is met.

©2010 Michelle Garcia Winner   www.socialthinking.com

Copyright©2010, Michelle Garcia Winner
All rights reserved. This book cannot be copied for the purposes of re-sale or sharing as an entire product.
This page may be copied for the purposes of educating students and other professionals.

Sticker Strategies: Practical Strategies to Encourage Social Thinking and Organization

EPS17.jpg

I Need a Break!

I really need to stop working for a few minutes and take a break. Once my body and brain calm back down I will rejoin the group and get back to work.

During my break I can go to: _____

I can do the following things:
_____

I need to avoid:
_____

©2010 Michelle Garcia Winner   www.socialthinking.com

EPS18.jpg

Emotion Summary:

I know my feelings change a lot each day.
I can calmly tell others how I feel right now:
Point to 1 or 2 emotions

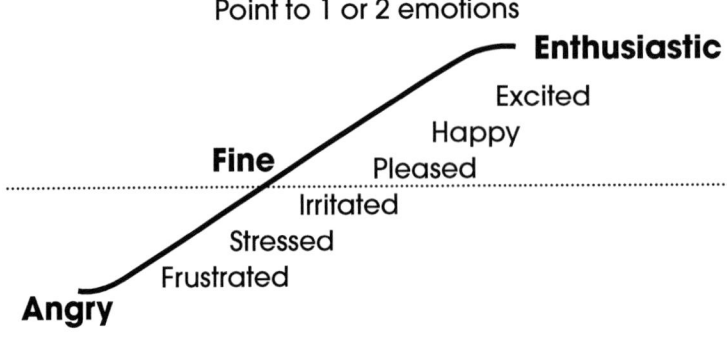

©2010 Michelle Garcia Winner   www.socialthinking.com

EPS19.jpg

Emotions:

Here are some things we know about emotions:

- We always feel some type of emotion.
- Our emotions change frequently throughout the day.
- We can use strategies to calm our emotions when they are feeling too big.
- By the time we are in school, we are not supposed to show our big negative emotions even if we feel them. We are supposed to calm ourselves down and calmly tell people how we feel even when we are feeling upset.

©2010 Michelle Garcia Winner   www.socialthinking.com

EPS20.jpg

Emotions are CONTAGIOUS!

If we are with people who are happy, we tend to feel happy. If we are with people who are sad, we tend to feel sad.

That also means if we are angry or mad, we may make others angry or mad. If we are happy and calm, we help people to stay happy and calm.

We can work together to help each other stay calm, even if things aren't perfect.

©2010 Michelle Garcia Winner   www.socialthinking.com

EPS21.jpg

We all have Emotions, but in the Classroom we Handle our Emotions by:

1. Describing them in a calm voice even when we are upset.
2. Pointing to our emotion on an emotion chart if we are too upset to speak.
3. Using calming strategies to help our brains refocus.

The job of every person in a group is to work to keep their emotions calm so the group can work together.

©2010 Michelle Garcia Winner   www.socialthinking.com

EPS22.jpg

The Spirals of Failure and Success
Understanding Social Anxiety and Social Ability:

Keeping yourself working to teach your brain to reach for your abilities!

- Self-doubt and excuses lead to failing to teach your brain new thinking (see The Spiral of Social Failure strategy)
- Willingness to try something that is uncomfortable by reassuring yourself you will be able to do it, leads to teaching your brain to try new things! (see The Spiral of Social Success strategy)

©2010 Michelle Garcia Winner   www.socialthinking.com

Emotions and Problem Solving

EPS23.jpg

EPS24.jpg

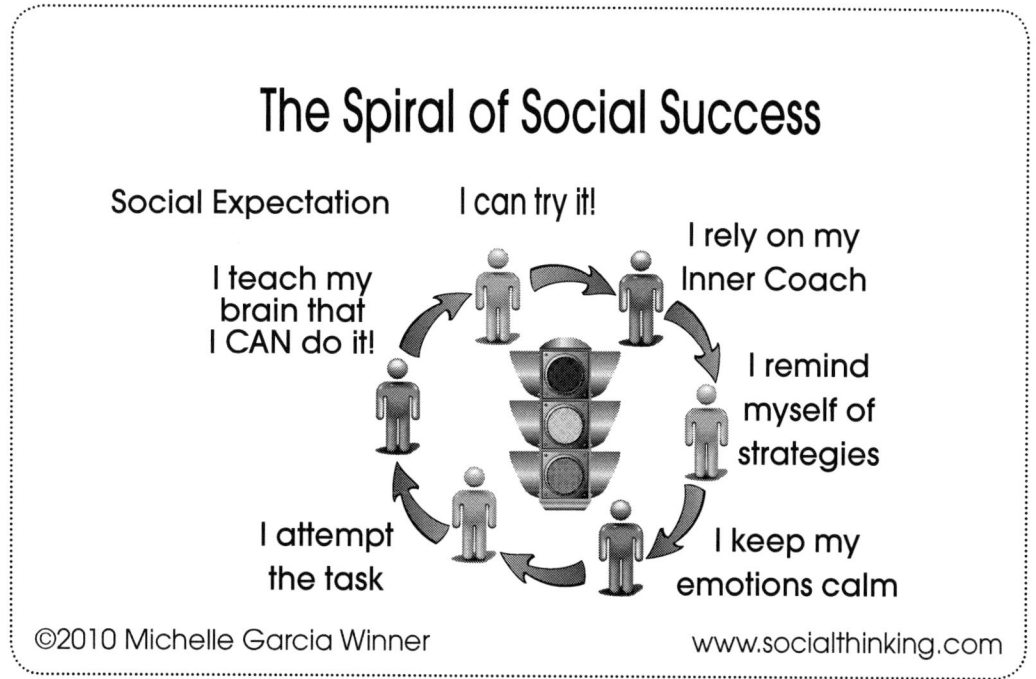

Sticker Strategies: Practical Strategies to Encourage Social Thinking and Organization

EPS-Blank.jpg

©2010 Michelle Garcia Winner   www.socialthinking.com

Organization, Writing, and Homework (O)

O1.jpg

Line-Thought: Strategy for Brainstorming

Use When:
- I am stuck when writing.
- I can't think of what to write.

Strategy:
- I can write my thoughts by drawing a short line and then adding my thought right after the line. It looks like this:
  — I like this idea.
  — I can do this.
  — I think one idea and write it briefly.
  — Then I write another!
  — It's called "line-thought."

©2010 Michelle Garcia Winner   www.socialthinking.com

O2.jpg

Get Started by...

1. Look at the board and listen to the teacher.
2. Look at what materials the other students have out.
3. Take out my own materials.
4. Organize my brain by:
   a. Reading directions
   b. Thinking about one thing at a time.
   c. Remind myself it will feel good when my work is done.
   d. Start to show my work so the teacher can see my thoughts.
   e. Ask for help if needed.

©2010 Michelle Garcia Winner   www.socialthinking.com

O3.jpg

Getting School Stuff Ready to Take Home:

1. Stop and Think about what has to be done tonight for homework.
2. Ask for help if I am not TOTALLY sure.
3. Review my notes to see what homework I have.
4. Figure out what textbooks I need to take home.
5. Figure out what binders I need to take home.
6. Figure out if there are any other books or handouts I need.
7. Stop and Organize my backpack so everything does not become smashed together.
8. I know that it takes time to get organized.

©2010 Michelle Garcia Winner   www.socialthinking.com

O4.jpg

Getting Started on Homework Once Home:

1. Get my homework materials together in one spot in the house.
   Fill out the list of things I keep near me when doing homework:

   a.

   b.

   c.

   d.

   e.

   f.

©2010 Michelle Garcia Winner   www.socialthinking.com

Sticker Strategies: Practical Strategies to Encourage Social Thinking and Organization

O5.jpg

Getting My Mind Organized to Start to do Homework:

Doing homework means thinking about what I am going to do:
1. Go to the bathroom.
2. Make sure I have relaxed a bit before starting homework.
3. Make a list of the different homework tasks I need to do.
4. Ask for help to clarify an assignment; call a friend!
5. Draw an asterisk next to the really important assignments on my list.
6. Make a smart guess about how long each assignment is going to take.
7. Figure out which order I should do my assignments in today. Indicate the order by numbering the list with a "1" for the first assignment, "2" for the second, etc..
8. Figure out when I get to take my first break.
9. Start doing the assignments once my mind has thought about what I need to do.

When I do it this way I am training my brain to think about ALL I have to do as well as EACH task I have to do!

©2010 Michelle Garcia Winner   www.socialthinking.com

O6.jpg

Starting to do the Homework:

1. Keep my brain focused on the task.
2. Remind myself I will feel good when the task is done.
3. Break down my task into smaller parts; for example if I have 15 math problems; pause after every 3 problems to tell myself that I am doing a good job.
4. Asking for help will keep me from getting too stressed out. Remind myself that I can get my work done better if I get some help. Everyone needs help sometimes.
5. Take a break during the time I promised myself I could break. For example, if I said I could get a break if I work steadily for 10 minutes, take a break when 10 minutes have passed.
6. Praise myself when I get back to work after my break has ended.

   By getting back to work I get my homework done.

©2010 Michelle Garcia Winner   www.socialthinking.com

Copyright©2010, Michelle Garcia Winner
All rights reserved. This book cannot be copied for the purposes of re-sale or sharing as an entire product.
This page may be copied for the purposes of educating students and other professionals.

O7.jpg

Homework Time is SET—
Free Time and Upset Time are FLEXIBLE:

There are certain times we have to do things;

There is time to do homework and time to have as free time.

Homework time is set and determined by how much homework I have.

Free time is always flexible, it changes depending on how much time I have available after I do my homework.

Upset time is also flexible, it changes depending on how much I can control it. When I get upset it usually takes time away from my free time.
My homework still takes the same amount of time.

Since I like my free time, I will try to focus on getting my homework done... because once I get it done I get more freetime!

©2010 Michelle Garcia Winner   www.socialthinking.com

O8.jpg

Breaking my Homework Assignments Down:

I can do my assignments best when I do parts of my assignments, one at a time.

When my assignments feel too big or too confusing, it means I need to break them apart and focus on only one step at a time.

For example, when I have to play a game, the first part is to set up the game, then to play the game, then to clean up the game.

©2010 Michelle Garcia Winner   www.socialthinking.com

O9.jpg

> ### Breaking my Homework Assignments Down:
>
> I can look at my homework by also breaking it into parts.
>
> 1. Set up my homework.
> 2. Break each homework assignment into parts; ask for help if I need help to figure out how to break my assignment into smaller parts.
> 3. Focus on only doing one part of my assignment at a time.
> 4. Congratulate myself each time I finish a part.
> 5. Figure out how many parts of an assignment I will do before I get to take a break away from the homework table for _____ minutes.
>
> ©2010 Michelle Garcia Winner   www.socialthinking.com

O10.jpg

> ### Why we Predict Time:
>
> All activities, fun or boring, happen while time passes.
>
> Each of us feel better if we know we can predict when we will be done with a task we don't like to do.
>
> With practice I will be able to predict how long each of my assignments will take, I will never predict perfectly well, but I will learn to make better smart guesses about how long I have to focus on each task.
>
> When I can make these predictions it will be easier for me to start a task knowing when it will most likely end.
>
> I can also look forward to what I get to do during my break when the task does end!
>
> ©2010 Michelle Garcia Winner   www.socialthinking.com

O11.jpg

Make a Game of Predicting Time:

Write 3 things you don't like to do. Then write down how long you think it will take to do each task. Then do each task, timing how long each actually takes. Write down how long it took. Find out if you over-estimate or under-estimate time on your predictions. Practice seeing if you can learn to get closer on your time predictions!

Task	My time prediction	My actual time to do the task

©2010 Michelle Garcia Winner   www.socialthinking.com

O12.jpg

Turning Homework In:

Once my homework assignment is completed at home, it is not considered "DONE" until I turn it in.

Even if I worked really hard on it, the teacher will have no idea I tried to do it if I don't turn it in.

If I cannot figure out when I am supposed to turn it in, I can:

a. Ask the teacher.

b. Ask another person in the class.

c. Give it to the teacher as soon as I enter into the class.

d. Or _____

If I don't turn it in, I may find the teachers are annoyed with me because they don't think I care about the class. Also, my parents are annoyed with me because they don't think I care about me!

When I turn in my homework I allow many people to be proud of me, including me.

©2010 Michelle Garcia Winner   www.socialthinking.com

013.jpg

Why Turn Homework In?

If I don't turn homework in:
- My teachers will not know that I did it.
- I also will not get any credit for it.
- My grade will go down, since part of my grade is for doing my homework.

Teachers also have feelings about their students. Students who don't turn in homework send a "silent message" that they don't care about the class. Teachers can interpret this message to also mean the student does not care about the teacher. Teachers may become frustrated with students who don't turn in their homework.

Parents also feel frustrated since they know their child did the work.

When I turn in my homework, I allow many people to be proud of me:

My teachers, my parents and ME!

©2010 Michelle Garcia Winner   www.socialthinking.com

014.jpg

Who Feels Good when my Homework is Done?

I feel good when my homework is done, since it is one less thing I have to do that I would rather not do!

My parents feel good when my homework is done since they see I am willing to work on things I don't like to do. They can also relax a bit more when I am not having to work so hard.

My teachers feel good when my homework is turned in since it shows I am participating in the class which makes the teacher feel good about me as a student in the class.

So, by doing my homework it makes many people feel good about me!

When people feel good about me it usually helps me to feel good about me!

©2010 Michelle Garcia Winner   www.socialthinking.com

Organization, Writing, and Homework (O)

O15.jpg

My Work and Break Card:

I will work or do my homework until:
_____

Then, I will take a break for: _____ minutes.

I promise not to go do an activity during break time that I have a hard time stopping once I get started
(e.g., like playing a computer game).

Congratulations on returning to the table!

I will come back to work and do more homework until:
_____

Then I will take another break for:

_____ minutes.

©2010 Michelle Garcia Winner www.socialthinking.com

O-Blank.jpg

©2010 Michelle Garcia Winner www.socialthinking.com

Group Work (GW)

GW1.jpg

Working in a Group and Being with People:
Working with other students in a group means I have to:
Keep my body, mind, and words in the group.

1. Move my body to join the group.
2. Share my ideas with the group, but don't expect them to accept them.
3. Acknowledge that other people have good ideas.
4. Agree to do PART of the work, but not ALL or NONE of it.
5. Make sure I do what I say I am going to do once I leave the group!
6. Allow for some time where people goof off in the group, this is called "networking."
7. Ask for clarification if I am confused about the assignment or about what other people are planning to do.
8. Get other people's email or phone number to contact them about the project from home.
9. Realize that most participants are feeling the project is a bit of a pain, even if they don't show it. Group work is complicated. Few people think it is truly fun. But they think, "when I have lemons, make lemonade".
10. Look forward to feeling good once the project is done and I have worked well with a team of people.

©2010 Michelle Garcia Winner   www.socialthinking.com

GW2.jpg

Starters for Working in a GROUP:
Working with other students in the group means I have to:
Keep my body, mind and words in the group!

1. Move my body to join the group!
2. Share my ideas with the group, but don't expect them to accept them.
3. Acknowledge that other people have good ideas too.
4. Agree to do PART of the work, but not ALL of it or NONE of it.

©2010 Michelle Garcia Winner   www.socialthinking.com

GW3.jpg

Pointless Work:

At school we do a lot of work that seems pointless and useless like "power writes" and "journal writes." There is sometimes no relevance or meaning to pointless work and we may never use it in the future, but we do it anyway to be part of a group. We have to do pointless work for the rest of our lives. Completing pointless work makes us feel successful and it makes us feel good about ourselves. I can also keep up with all of my work!

So, when it comes to pointless work: JUST DO IT!

©2010 Michelle Garcia Winner www.socialthinking.com

GW4.jpg

Thinking about Social Behavior Mapping:

Behavior ➡ affects feelings ➡ affects how people treat me ➡ affects how I feel about myself and how I feel about others.

1. My behavior makes people have thoughts and feelings.
2. People's feelings are usually positive if my behavior is expected; their feelings are usually negative if my behavior is unexpected.
3. How people feel contributes to how they treat me.
   a. If they feel bad about my behavior, they will treat me less kindly.
   b. If they feel good about my behavior, they will treat me with more kindness.
4. How people treat me affects how I feel about myself.
   a. If people treat me well, I feel good about myself.
   b. If people treat me poorly, I feel bad about myself.

©2010 Michelle Garcia Winner www.socialthinking.com

GW5.jpg

Boring Moment Expectations:

When I am in a group of two or more people, I risk getting a bit bored. It is expected that I will be bored part of the time I am in a group. Here are some EXPECTED behaviors I DO when I am bored:

- Keep my body and eyes turned toward the teacher or group.
- Keep my comments focused on the topic.
- Fidget or doodle quietly without distracting others or even myself from what is going on around me.
- Keep my classwork on my desk.
- Keep my negative thoughts to myself.
- Stay alert to the group so I can jump back into the discussion without looking like I wasn't paying attention.
- Continue to sit up in my chair.
- Keep my hands and feet to myself.

©2010 Michelle Garcia Winner www.socialthinking.com

GW6.jpg

Doing What is UNEXPECTED when I am Having a Boring Moment

When I am in a group of two or more people, I risk getting a bit bored. It is expected that I will be bored part of the time I am in a group. If I do UNEXPECTED behaviors when I am bored I am likely to get myself in trouble or to make people around me have "weird thoughts." Unexpected behaviors include:

- Wandering around the classroom or away from the social group.
- Sleeping or looking like I am sleeping.
- Distracting others with my body or words.
- Talking about things not related to the topic or class work.
- Telling other people what they are doing is wrong.
- Taking trips to the bathroom or pencil sharpener.
- Reading books during class time that are not related to class work.
- Turning my body and eyes away from the teacher or group.
- Announcing I am bored or that I already know all the information!

©2010 Michelle Garcia Winner www.socialthinking.com

Copyright©2010, Michelle Garcia Winner
All rights reserved. This book cannot be copied for the purposes of re-sale or sharing as an entire product.
This page may be copied for the purposes of educating students and other professionals.

Group Work

GW-Blank.jpg

©2010 Michelle Garcia Winner	www.socialthinking.com

ST1.jpg

Being Social:

"Your friends are people who make you feel good about you!"

©2010 Michelle Garcia Winner   www.socialthinking.com

ST2.jpg

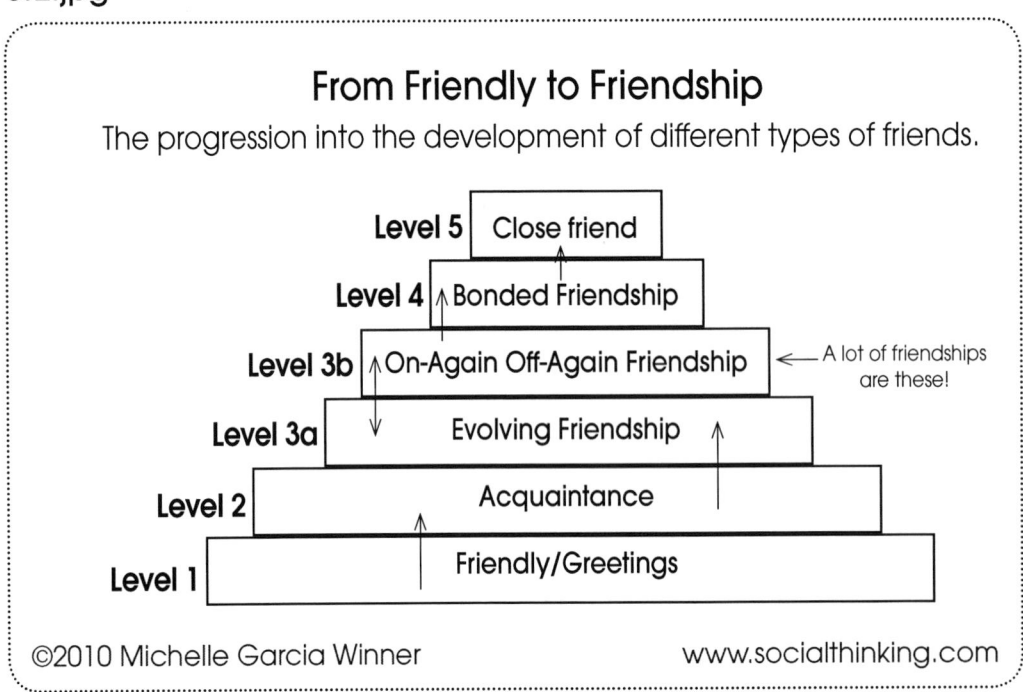

From Friendly to Friendship
The progression into the development of different types of friends.

- Level 5 — Close friend
- Level 4 — Bonded Friendship
- Level 3b — On-Again Off-Again Friendship ← A lot of friendships are these!
- Level 3a — Evolving Friendship
- Level 2 — Acquaintance
- Level 1 — Friendly/Greetings

©2010 Michelle Garcia Winner   www.socialthinking.com

Social Thinking

ST3.jpg

Levels of Friendship

Level 1 Greetings: Saying "Hi" to show you are friendly, even if you don't know the person well or at all. By saying "Hi" you demonstrate to people you welcome people to talk to you.

Level 2 Acquaintance: People you happen to talk to, you don't plan to talk to them because you really don't know them yet. An acquaintance may be a friend-of-a-friend or a person you sit next to in class or stand near in line.

Level 3a Evolving Friendship: Someone you have likely met as an acquaintance but now you seek them out with the purpose of hanging out in the same general place you first met them. If you met them in school then you ask if they want to have lunch with you at school. You may Facebook friend them.

©2010 Michelle Garcia Winner   www.socialthinking.com

ST4.jpg

Levels of Friendship

Step 3b On again - off again friend: Once this person is an evolving, bonded or close friend they may not always be a friend to you. They may be more of a friend during one period of time than another; their friendship fades. For example, you were friends with them when you had a class together, but the friendship faded when the class ended. Not all friends are friends for life!

Level 4 Bonded friend: These are friends who do things together away from where they first met. If they met at school they now arrange to meet at their houses, in the community, etc. They go out of their way to arrange time to be with each other to do things like go to movies, play video games, shop, etc.

©2010 Michelle Garcia Winner   www.socialthinking.com

Copyright©2010, Michelle Garcia Winner
All rights reserved. This book cannot be copied for the purposes of re-sale or sharing as an entire product.
This page may be copied for the purposes of educating students and other professionals.

ST5.jpg

Levels of Friendship

Level 5 Very close friend: This person is a bonded friend with more intensity. This is the person you trust to tell some of your private thoughts and feelings to. You can enjoy being with this person without having to talk all the time. We describe this as "being there for each other."

©2010 Michelle Garcia Winner   www.socialthinking.com

ST6.jpg

When do we use Social Skills?

We use social skills any time we are near people to help them understand we are thinking socially about how to behave in different settings and with different people. Our social skills help people to know we are thinking about them and their feelings.

©2010 Michelle Garcia Winner   www.socialthinking.com

ST7.jpg

The Four Steps of Social Thinking/Perspective Taking:

When Sharing Space I need to Realize That...

Step 1: All people have little thoughts about the people around them, even if they have no plans to communicate with them.

Step 2: All people try to figure out "why are you near me" and/or "why are you saying this to me?"

Step 3: Since I know you are thinking about me, I try to figure out what you are thinking about me.

Step 4: So..I monitor and possibly modify my behavior to keep you thinking about me the way I want you to think about me.

©2010 Michelle Garcia Winner   www.socialthinking.com

ST8.jpg

Perspective Taking
Step 1: All people have thoughts

All people have little thoughts.

They are aware the person is having a thought about them as well!

We cannot avoid having thoughts about people around us, being aware of people keeps us safe.

Knowing that we all have thoughts about each other, we seem "wired" to want people to have "good thoughts" rather than "weird thoughts" about us.

©2010 Michelle Garcia Winner   www.socialthinking.com

ST9.jpg

Perspective Taking
Step 2: Motive/Intent

Since people are having thoughts, their first thought is to figure out your motives or intentions; they try to *read your plan* by thinking, "what are you planning to do next?"

Again, this is for our safety, our brains try and figure out what people are planning to do when they are near us so we can figure out if they are safe to have near us.

This thinking also helps us to figure out who is friendly and whether they are pursuing a friendship with us or whether they are trying to trick us. Figuring this out gets harder and harder as people start to be very subtle about their intentions past 3rd grade.

©2010 Michelle Garcia Winner   www.socialthinking.com

ST10.jpg

Perspective Taking
Step 3: Considering their thoughts

Given we know people have little thoughts about us, we should wonder what they might be thinking.

We are constantly considering what other people are thinking about us, this is normal behavior even as young as preschool and kindergarten!

©2010 Michelle Garcia Winner   www.socialthinking.com

ST11.jpg

Perspective Taking
Step 4: Modifying our behavior?

Given that we are figuring out what people might be thinking about us, we constantly monitor and possibly change our behavior to try and keep people having pretty good or even just bland thoughts about us.

We should modify our behavior to help people avoid having "weird" thoughts about us. When people have weird thoughts about us, we attract attention to ourselves. People remember things that are thought of as "weird" far more often than they remember when we do something that is considered "normal."

©2010 Michelle Garcia Winner   www.socialthinking.com

ST12.jpg

Social Emotional Memory

We have to be aware people have a "social-emotional memory." They decide who to hangout with or treat nicely based on what types of memories they have about us.

Most students will be more likely to want to be friends with someone who gives them good memories. Students form knowledge of other students in classes, even if they never have talked to the student.

Remember, we are always aware of who is around us even if we are not talking to them.

©2010 Michelle Garcia Winner   www.socialthinking.com

ST13.jpg

Feelings Count!

We cannot avoid having feelings. Every one of us has feelings all of the time.

How we make someone feel counts. People consider others to be "cool" if they make us feel calm and safe in their presence.

People have feelings about people they don't even talk to. Thoughts lead to feelings.

We even have feelings in math and science classes!

Your feelings also count; you will only want to be with people who make you feel good about you!

©2010 Michelle Garcia Winner   www.socialthinking.com

ST14.jpg

Calling People Even if you have Phone Anxiety!

Calling people shows you are interested in them; that you are thinking about them.

If someone is friendly to you at school and they give you their phone number and you DON'T call, they then think that you don't really like them!

A lot of teens call each other just to ask, "What's up" and then to tell something about their own day. This just shows that they are interested in talking to the person.

What you actually say in the conversation is more about being "friendly" than it is about showing you are "smart."

Social language is about connecting to how people feel; classroom discussions are more about demonstrating your knowledge.

©2010 Michelle Garcia Winner   www.socialthinking.com

ST15.jpg

The Four Steps of Communication:

1. Think about the other person, what you know about them, and what he or she is feeling.

2. Be aware of your physical presence as well as the presence of others.

3. Use your eyes to think about others and see what they are thinking about.

4. Use your language to relate to others.

©2010 Michelle Garcia Winner   www.socialthinking.com

ST16.jpg

Communication
Step 1: Think about Others

Think about the other person and what he or she is thinking/feeling:

a. Ask myself: What are the people near me interested in?

b. Do I remember something about them?

c. How do they feel about what I am saying?

d. How do they feel about what I am doing?

e. What am I doing and saying to show I am interested in the persons I am with?

©2010 Michelle Garcia Winner   www.socialthinking.com

ST17.jpg

Communication
Step 2: Physical Presence

Be aware of my physical presence as well as the physical presence of others. This alters, in part, how we feel about each other.

a. My body position shows who I want to talk to or who I don't want to talk to.

b. My body movements show what I plan to do next. This communicates messages to people even if I am not communicating directly.

c. My body language, physical stance, relaxed or rigid posture and facial expression is interpreted to communicate how I feel about the situation and people around me. People usually like to be with people who show more relaxed body language.

©2010 Michelle Garcia Winner   www.socialthinking.com

ST18.jpg

Communication
Step 3: Eyes are for Thinking

I use my eyes to think about what other people are thinking and feeling.

a. The direction of a person's eyes lets others see what they might be thinking about.

b. We use our eyes to help figure out how other people feel, their possible thoughts and if they are interested in the other people they are with.

©2010 Michelle Garcia Winner   www.socialthinking.com

ST19.jpg

Communication
Step 4: Relate to People

I use my language to relate to others, rather than to just tell them about myself.

a. Talk about things that are interesting to others by asking questions to find out what they are interested in or by making comments related to what they are talking about.

b. Add my own thoughts or describe my own experiences to connect to other people's ideas. People like it when my thoughts show an extension of what they were thinking.

c. If I enter a group of people, enter silently, listening to what they are talking about. Adjust my language to what the group or other people are talking about.

©2010 Michelle Garcia Winner   www.socialthinking.com

ST-Blank.jpg

©2010 Michelle Garcia Winner   www.socialthinking.com

Family Time – Home Strategies (FT)

FT1.jpg

Family Dinner Time: Answering Questions

Your parents like it when you show you are thinking about them.

When they ask, "What did you do at school today?" think of one activity you did in one class and explain it.

We talk about information not because it is fascinating, but because by telling a little bit about our lives we let people learn about what we do and feel.

©2010 Michelle Garcia Winner   www.socialthinking.com

FT2.jpg

Family Dinner Time: Asking Questions

Your parents like it when you show you are thinking about them.

When you ask a question to a person at the table about their day, it shows you are interested in them and that makes people feel good.

Here are some simple conversation starters:

1. Did you have a good day?
2. What did you do today?

©2010 Michelle Garcia Winner   www.socialthinking.com

FT3.jpg

Family Dinner Time:
Add your own Thoughts

When other people are talking at the table, you are part of the group. They expect you to be listening and adding in your own connected thought.

For example, if you hear your family talking about TV shows and homework in one discussion, any related comment you make on these topics would likely be good. For example, tell the name of a show you like to watch.

Avoid making just negative comments about other people's experiences. For example if someone describes a favorite TV show, avoid announcing that you HATE that show. People don't like it when someone makes their ideas sound bad.

©2010 Michelle Garcia Winner   www.socialthinking.com

FT4.jpg

After Dinner is Done:
HELP OUT

The adults in the house that helped to prepare dinner have had a long day and they are tired.

At the end of dinner, do your part to help the group by clearing your dishes and helping to put away some food, WITHOUT being asked to help.

This probably takes no more than 5 minutes to help out and it makes a lasting good memory in the mind of the adult you are helping.

When people feel good about you they treat you more kindly.

©2010 Michelle Garcia Winner   www.socialthinking.com

FT5.jpg

Sharing the TV:

Many houses only have one TV in the house that has to be shared. Brothers and sisters often do not like to watch the same TV shows.

Unexpected behavior when not everyone in the room agrees on what show to watch:

1. Screaming at each other.
2. Throwing the remote control.
3. Walking into the room and turning the channel when one person is already watching the TV.
4. Turning off the TV when someone else is watching it.
5. Physically fighting.

©2010 Michelle Garcia Winner   www.socialthinking.com

FT6.jpg

Sharing the TV:

Expected behavior when not everyone in the room agrees on what show to watch:

1. If you enter the room and someone is already watching a show, ask if you can pick the next show to watch.
2. Think of other things you can do while the person finishes watching the show (e.g., play on the computer, read a book, draw, etc.).
3. Watch the show that is on so you have something you can talk about with the person who is watching the show you don't prefer.
4. Stay calm by remembering, the level of this problem is about 1 or 2 on the problem solving scale, which means the level of your emotions should stay relatively calm.

©2010 Michelle Garcia Winner   www.socialthinking.com

Copyright©2010, Michelle Garcia Winner
All rights reserved. This book cannot be copied for the purposes of re-sale or sharing as an entire product.
This page may be copied for the purposes of educating students and other professionals.

FT7.jpg

Ending an Activity when Asked:

Each of us REALLY likes to do certain activities. However, free time does not mean we are always free to do whatever we want.

Free time is unstructured time that needs to be structured.

When planning to enjoy a free time activity of your choosing, you have to start by deciding what time you have to STOP doing the activity.

Usually you have to STOP because there are other things that you have to do (even if they are not as much fun) such as homework, chores or getting ready for bed.

Sometimes your parents want you to STOP just because your brain needs to think about a variety of things and they feel your brain is STUCK thinking only about what is fun for you.

It is BEST for you to STOP your activity of choice before people feel like they have to NAG you to stop. Once they NAG you they are IRRITATED.

Your parents should give you a 5 minute warning to STOP to give your brain a chance to wind down. However, you MUST STOP once the time is up, or else you are bound to get in an argument. Arguments never make anyone feel good.

©2010 Michelle Garcia Winner   www.socialthinking.com

FT8.jpg

Getting Ready for Bed:

Our brains like routine. Getting ready for bed each night should be a routine. My brain has to settle down and calm down to allow for sleep.

Write out your bed time routine:

1. _____

2. _____

3. _____

4. _____

Routines need to be followed to be remembered. Follow your bedtime routine.

©2010 Michelle Garcia Winner   www.socialthinking.com

FT9.jpg

People Think about how you Smell

People have thoughts about people even when they are not talking to them. They have thoughts about how they look, if their teeth are clean, if their hair looks cared for, if they smell, etc.

The hidden rule is that we do not tell people when we have weird thoughts about their hygiene. However, if someone is having a weird thought about another's hygiene – they often go tell 10 of their friends.

Each of us is responsible for keeping our body, teeth, hair, nails, and clothing clean and cared for not only for our own health, but also because it helps us to avoid other people's "weird thoughts."

©2010 Michelle Garcia Winner   www.socialthinking.com

FT10.jpg

Getting up in the Morning:

We have to think about 3 things to get us going in the morning:

1. NO ONE thinks it feels good to have to get out of bed from a deep sleep.
2. Getting ready for school takes time.
3. ALL students have to get to school at a specific time.

Which means:

We all force ourselves to get up in the morning, even though it feels awful, in order to have the time to get ready for school so we can get to school on time.

You are just like everyone else. You just have to keep focused on why you have to get up rather than the fact you don't want to get up.

©2010 Michelle Garcia Winner   www.socialthinking.com

FT11.jpg

Morning Routine:

All of us should have a morning routine that includes getting out of bed by a specific time, taking care of our hygiene and living space, eating breakfast, and planning time to get to school.

Write out the steps of your routine below:

1. _____
2. _____
3. _____
4. _____
5. _____
6. _____

By following routines it helps my brain to get organized and be more successful each day.

©2010 Michelle Garcia Winner   www.socialthinking.com

FT12.jpg

Parents are People Too!

All people have thoughts and emotions, even parents.

Parents have good days and bad days. Parents have joys and frustrations.

Parents will react in a bad way to things and people that make them feel bad.

Parents will react in a good way to things and people that make them feel good.

Parents are the most enjoyable to be with when they are calm and in a good mood. However, their good moods don't usually just happen, they are created by the people and situations around them.

If you want your parents to stay calm and be happy, think of 2 things you can do to help keep them feeling like that.

1. _____
2. _____

©2010 Michelle Garcia Winner   www.socialthinking.com

FT13.jpg

Apologizing:

Each of us makes mistakes. That is what is meant by saying, we are just "Being Human."

Since we are going to say and do things that make people feel bad at times, the way we help to fix the bad feelings is by apologizing.

When you are little you just walk up to the person and you say, "I am sorry." But when you get older (3rd grade and older), just saying you're sorry is not enough. Now people expect you to show you are sorry through your behavior. Ways we show people we are sorry, in addition to saying we are sorry, include:

1. Letting the person we offended choose what game or activity we are going to do next.
2. Complimenting the person.
3. Listening to what the person has to say and finding points where we can agree with them.
4. Allowing them to share their ideas without telling them they are wrong or that you know more than they do.
5. Having a calm and relaxed happy face when they talk (not looking angry at them).
6. Laughing subtly when they tell a joke.

What else can you think of?

©2010 Michelle Garcia Winner   www.socialthinking.com

FT14.jpg

Social Memories of Parents:

Think about the fact that YOU remember how people make YOU feel!

Most people remember not only facts, but also information about people that they know. We REMEMBER HOW PEOPLE MAKE US FEEL more than we remember what people told us.

EVEN YOUR PARENTS REMEMBER HOW YOU HAVE MADE THEM FEEL.

We choose who we want to spend our time with based on who makes us feel good. Most people would not choose to spend time with someone that makes them feel bad.

This is why each one of us has to learn to monitor our own behavior and words and think about how they are making the other person feel.

©2010 Michelle Garcia Winner   www.socialthinking.com

Copyright©2010, Michelle Garcia Winner
All rights reserved. This book cannot be copied for the purposes of re-sale or sharing as an entire product.
This page may be copied for the purposes of educating students and other professionals.

FT15.jpg

Taking my Medications:

Each of us has a brain that is not perfect. Some times our brains make us more anxious, or worried or sad than seems fair.

Doctors have developed medications to help our brains find balance.

We are given medications to help either our body or our brain feel better. We need to take our medications to be fair to ourselves.

I will take my medication every day. I will learn how my medication helps my brain or body so I understand why it is so important for me to take.

My medication routine is:

Medication	Reason I take this	Time of day I take it	Amount I take
1.			
2.			
3.			

When I follow my routine it helps my brain to remember what to do!

©2010 Michelle Garcia Winner   www.socialthinking.com

FT16.jpg

Life is Not Fair

Enjoying things we like to do, seeing sights we like to see, and being with people who make us feel good are some of the reasons we enjoy life.

But life is not just about enjoyment, it is also about having to do things we don't want to do in order to learn to take care of ourselves.

Sometimes life is just no fun at all. We have to do work or chores that don't make us feel good, but they are what is expected. We do these to either help other people or to help us learn to work as part of a group.

Sometimes life seems unfair. It seems like someone else gets something better than us. However, remember there are times when you get good things other people don't get.

Life is not about being fair, it is about balancing our pleasures with the boring or even the frustrating moments.

Avoid getting stuck in the bad moment, instead remember things will improve and you will feel better soon again.

We have a saying, "when you have lemons, make lemonade."

©2010 Michelle Garcia Winner   www.socialthinking.com

FT17.jpg

Doing Chores:

Doing chores around the house not only helps to teach you how to care for your own living space one day, but it also takes some of the burden away from your parent(s) having to do everything.

Chores do not usually take very long to do. For example, taking out the trash takes less than 5 minutes in most houses; starting a load of laundry takes about 3 minutes; putting on a new toilet paper roll takes about 45 seconds. YOU HAVE TIME TO DO CHORES.

If you don't do the chore you've been asked to do, then who is going to do it? Your parents have a lot to do in their lives and when you help them out it makes them feel good and proud of you. It also helps them avoid worrying about whether you will ever figure out how to be a "team player" which in part means you do unpleasant tasks just to make someone else feel better.

Remember: it takes LESS TIME to do the chores than to ARGUE about doing the chores.

©2010 Michelle Garcia Winner   www.socialthinking.com

FT18.jpg

Making my Chores Routine:

I help my family by doing chores. I can make chores part of my routine.

Below I have listed my chore routine.

Chore	Time of day I will do it	Amount of time it takes to do the chore

When I do the chore my family is proud of me. When people feel good about me, I feel good about myself.

Doing the chores in my house makes my parents have a good social memory of me.

©2010 Michelle Garcia Winner   www.socialthinking.com

Family Time – Home Strategies

FT-Blank.jpg

©2010 Michelle Garcia Winner   www.socialthinking.com

Also by Michelle Garcia Winner and Think Social Publishing, Inc.

Think Social! A Social Thinking Curriculum for School Aged Students

Inside Out! What Makes a Person with Social Cognitive Deficits Tick?

Thinking About YOU Thinking About ME, 2nd edition

Social Behavior Mapping:
Connecting Behavior, Emotions and Consequences Across the Day
Available in English and Spanish

Superflex... A Superhero Social Thinking Curriculum
(co-authored by Stephanie Madrigal)

Superflex takes on Glassman and the Team of Unthinkables
(co-authored by Stephanie Madrigal)

You are a Social Detective!
(co-authored by Pamela Crooke) Available in English, French, and Spanish

Worksheets for Teaching Social Thinking and Related Skills

Strategies for Organization: Preparing for Homework and the Real World

Social Thinking Across the Home and School Day

Social Thinking Posters for Home and the Classroom

A Politically Incorrect Look at Evidence-based Practices and Teaching Social Skills: A Literature Review and Discussion

Socially Curious and Curiously Social:
A Social Thinking Guidebook for Teens and Young Adults

We Can Make It Better! Stories©
By Elizabeth M. Delsandro

Please go to www.socialthinking.com for a full list of our products and resources.